CBT Toolbox for Kids

101 Fun Activities and Exercises to Help Children Deal with Difficult Emotions, Conquer Worries, and Develop Healthy Habits

© Copyright 2023 - All rights reserved.

The content contained within this book may not be reproduced, duplicated, or transmitted without direct written permission from the author or the publisher.

Under no circumstances will any blame or legal responsibility be held against the publisher or author for any damages, reparation, or monetary loss due to the information contained within this book, either directly or indirectly.

Legal Notice:

This book is copyright-protected. It is only for personal use. You cannot amend, distribute, sell, use, quote, or paraphrase any part of the content within this book without the consent of the author or publisher.

Disclaimer Notice:

Please note the information contained within this document is for educational and entertainment purposes only. All effort has been executed to present accurate, up-to-date, reliable, and complete information. No warranties of any kind are declared or implied. Readers acknowledge that the author is not engaging in the rendering of legal, financial, medical, or professional advice. The content within this book has been derived from various sources. Please consult a licensed professional before attempting any techniques outlined in this book.

By reading this document, the reader agrees that under no circumstances is the author responsible for any losses, direct or indirect, that are incurred as a result of the use of the information contained within this document, including, but not limited to, errors, omissions, or inaccuracies.

Table of Contents

INTRODUCTION LETTER TO PARENTS 1
INTRODUCTION LETTER TO CHILDREN 2
SECTION 1: WHAT AM I FEELING? 3
SECTION 2: EXPRESSING MYSELF 21
SECTION 3: TAMING MY FEARS 31
SECTION 4: PUTTING MY ANGER TO SLEEP 40
SECTION 5: KEEPING MY WORRIES AWAY 46
SECTION 6: ANXIETY FIGHTERS 52
SECTION 7: MY ZEN ZONE 61
SECTION 8: HEALTHY HABITS, HAPPY MINDS 66
SECTION 9: CONQUERING MY BIGGEST CHALLENGES 72
SECTION 10: EMBRACING MYSELF 79
BONUS SECTION: THOUGHT CHALLENGE 86
THANK YOU 88
CHECK OUT ANOTHER BOOK IN THE SERIES 89
REFERENCES 90

Introduction Letter to Parents

Dear Parents,

This book is a comprehensive CBT toolbox for children. CBT stands for Cognitive Behavioral Therapy, a therapeutic protocol that helps with various problems, including anxiety and depression. The tools outlined in the exercises will equip your child with the skills needed to form strong relationships, solve problems, and regulate their emotions.

By working through these exercises, your child will be given skills that can be applied throughout their life. The CBT activities are structured in such a way as to incorporate mental, physical, and emotional well-being. Many adults do not know how to work through their emotions and traumatic experiences. This lack of understanding of their minds can lead to adverse outcomes. Your desire to protect your child is admirable, but you cannot be there all the time. Therefore, the exercises here are created in a way that lays the foundation for independence and helps instill critical thinking and emotional intelligence, which are needed to navigate a volatile world.

Introduction Letter to Children

Dear Children,

Sometimes, life can get tough and be very confusing. You will experience moments when the confusion of life causes you to be angry, annoyed, frustrated, and unhappy. This book gives you the tools you need to make positive changes to help you feel better about yourself and your relationships with your friends and family.

There is a lot that happens in the world that you cannot control. You must learn to accept what you can and cannot control. One of the things you have control over is your mind. This book teaches you how your mind works and how you can use your mind to become a better person and achieve all your dreams. By completing all these exercises, you will realize how much potential you have and how much you can change the world just by being yourself.

Section 1: What Am I Feeling?

Do you know what feelings are?

When you are having fun with your friends, you will feel happy. If you get into an argument with one of your classmates, you will feel angry.

Feelings are all the different ways that people can feel on the inside. People feel good when things they like happen, and they feel bad when things do not go their way.

Another word for feelings is emotions. Your emotions change all the time during the day. Some emotions stay around longer than others.

Notebook or Copybook Journal

Before you begin, ask your parents for a notebook or a copybook journal. This book will help you do many of the exercises in this book. Enjoy!

Exercise 1

Sometimes, you feel like there is a storm in your stomach that does not feel good at all. At other times, you feel warm and fuzzy.

All these feelings are part of being human. If you understand how you are feeling, you can make better choices about how you react.

Can you draw a picture of how you are feeling right now?

Exercise 2

When you speak to other people like your friends, family, and teachers, you can make them feel good or bad depending on how you treat them.

Sometimes, your friend may be sad and could use your help to feel better. At other times, your friend may be happy, which means it's a great time to have fun together!

Looking at people's faces and bodies can tell you a lot about how they are feeling today.

Can you label which feelings listed here match the faces shown below?

Angry. Happy. Sad. Frustrated. Disgusted. Surprised. Shy. Scared.

Exercise 3

It can be difficult to talk about how you feel.

When you do not have the words to label how you feel, you can describe your emotions so that people around you know how their actions and behavior may affect you.

You can tell people how you feel by letting them know what is happening in your body when you feel a type of emotion. Write down how your body feels inside or what your body does when you are:

- Angry
- Happy
- Sad
- Frustrated
- Disgusted
- Surprised
- Shy
- Scared

Happy.

Sad.

Angry.

Frustrated. *(Feeling frustrated means that you are annoyed because you cannot change something that is not going the way you want it to.)*

Surprised.

Disgusted. *(Being disgusted is the feeling people get when something is gross.)*

Shy.

Scared.

Exercise 4

Let's play a game of pretend. The following stories describe different situations. Draw a picture of how each story made you feel.

Your friend found a frog in your backyard. They ask you if you want to touch the frog and hold it close to you.

Your friend found a frog.
https://pixabay.com/vectors/frog-toad-water-green-frog-6026117/

You fell off a bicycle, and your friends laughed at you.

Falling off your bicycle might cause negative feelings.
https://pixabay.com/vectors/bicycle-small-vehicle-bike-cycle-1456759/

Your parents bought you your favorite toy for your birthday.

Birthdays are a cause for celebration.
https://pixabay.com/vectors/cake-candles-birthday-purple-icing-308576/

You are on a rollercoaster that is going very fast.

Rollercoasters can be very fast.

https://pixabay.com/vectors/rollercoaster-roller-coaster-156027/

Your brother, sister, or friend ate some of your Halloween candy when you were not looking.

Trick-or-treating can help you collect a lot of candy.
https://pixabay.com/vectors/pumpkin-halloween-jack-o-lantern-2504236/

You are late on your first day of school.

Schools can help you learn.

https://pixabay.com/vectors/school-building-education-property-295210/

Exercise 5

What is your favorite color?

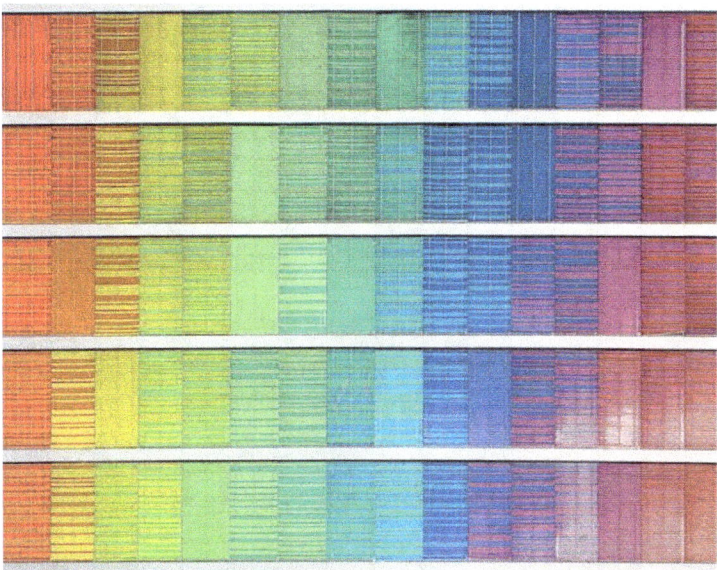

People can have the same favorite color

https://unsplash.com/photos/pRZVCSTqje4?utm_source=unsplash&utm_medium=referral&utm_content=creditShareLink

That's a great color! Some people like your favorite color, too. Other people do not like it as much as you do, and that's fine.

Can you write down how these colors make you feel?

Exercise 6

Sometimes, your feelings can feel quite big, like a giant elephant.

Your feelings can feel as big as an elephant.

https://pixabay.com/vectors/elephant-animal-jungle-savannah-1598359/

Sometimes your feelings can be very teeny-tiny, like a little bitty mouse.

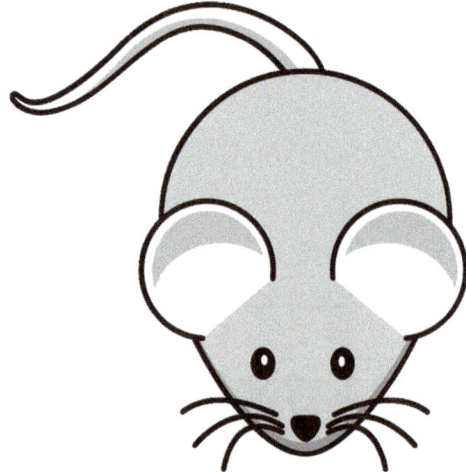

Your feelings can also feel as tiny as a mouse.

https://pixabay.com/vectors/mouse-grey-mammal-rodent-whiskers-303878/

Some things make you happy, and other things can make you sad. Some things can make you very sad, and other things can make you a little bit sad.

How big or small your feelings are is known as intensity. Big feelings are very intense. Small feelings are not so intense. Color in how intense your feelings are for each of the following stories.

Green = Not intense.

Orange = A little intense.

Yellow = Medium intense.

Red = Very intense.

Your friend or sibling hid the TV remote from you. Write down how you felt. Color in how intense that feeling is using green, yellow, orange, or red.

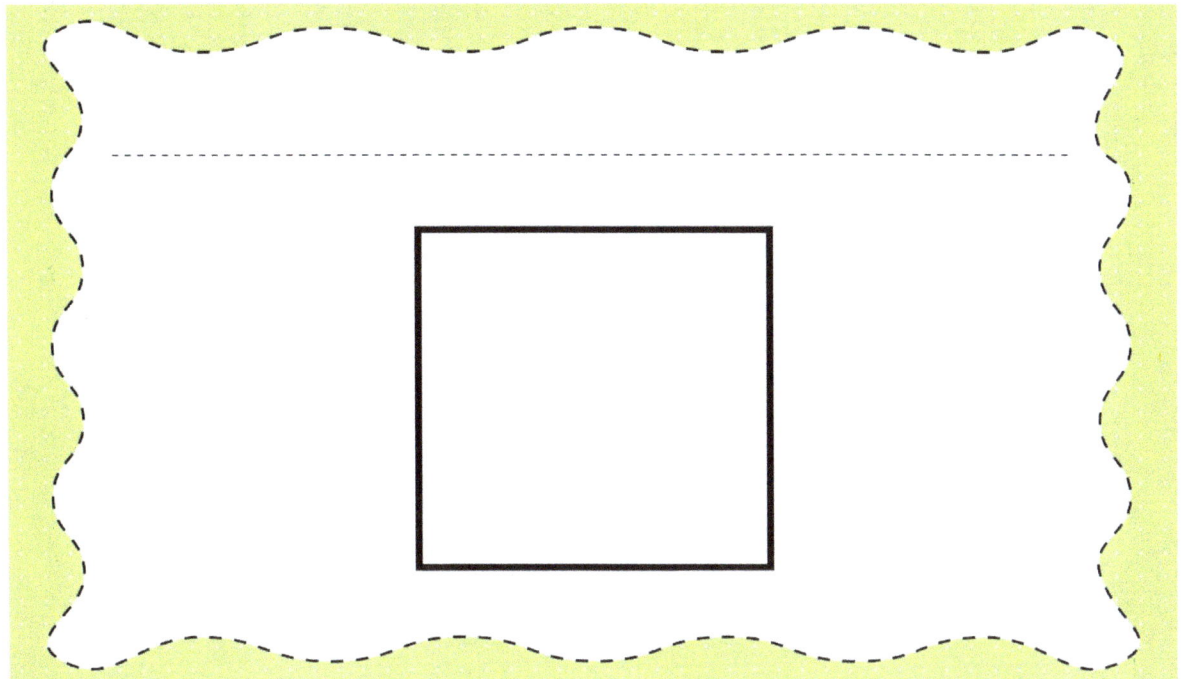

The ice cream cone that you just bought falls on the ground. Write down how you feel. Color in how intense that feeling is using green, yellow, orange, or red.

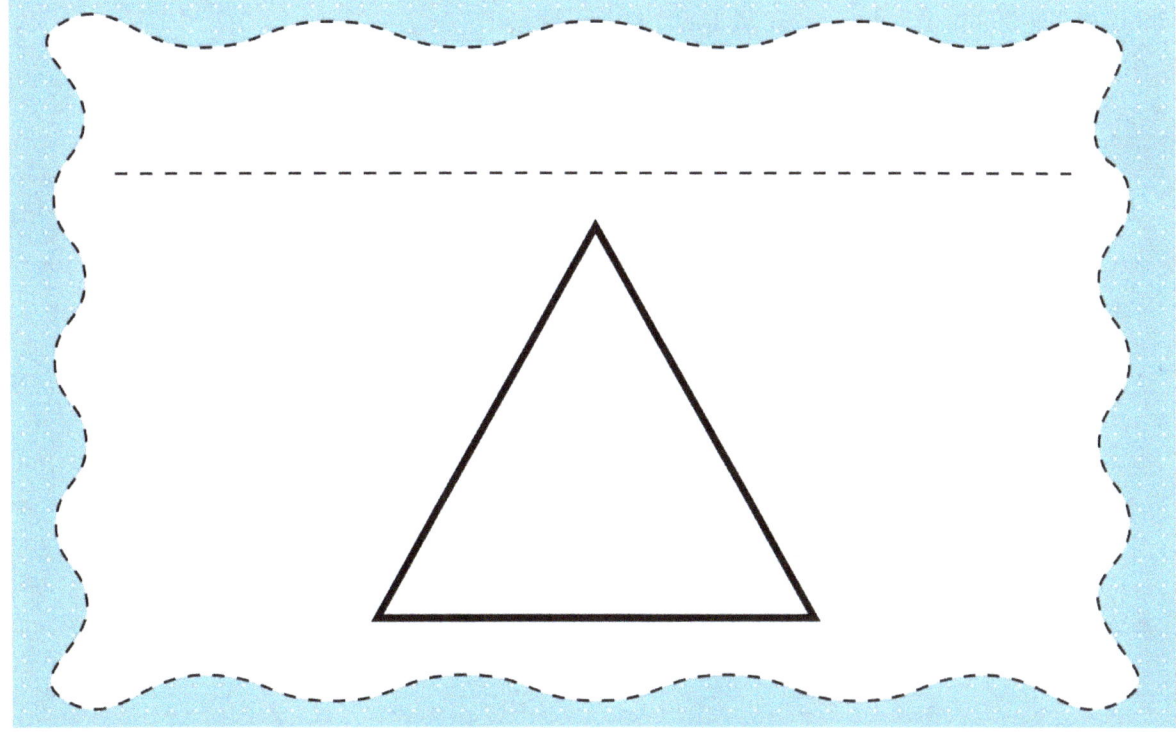

Your teacher or your parents yell at you for misbehaving. Write down how you feel. Color in how intense that feeling is using green, yellow, orange, or red.

You are playing a video game with your friend, and you lose. Write down how you feel. Color in how intense that feeling is using green, yellow, orange, or red.

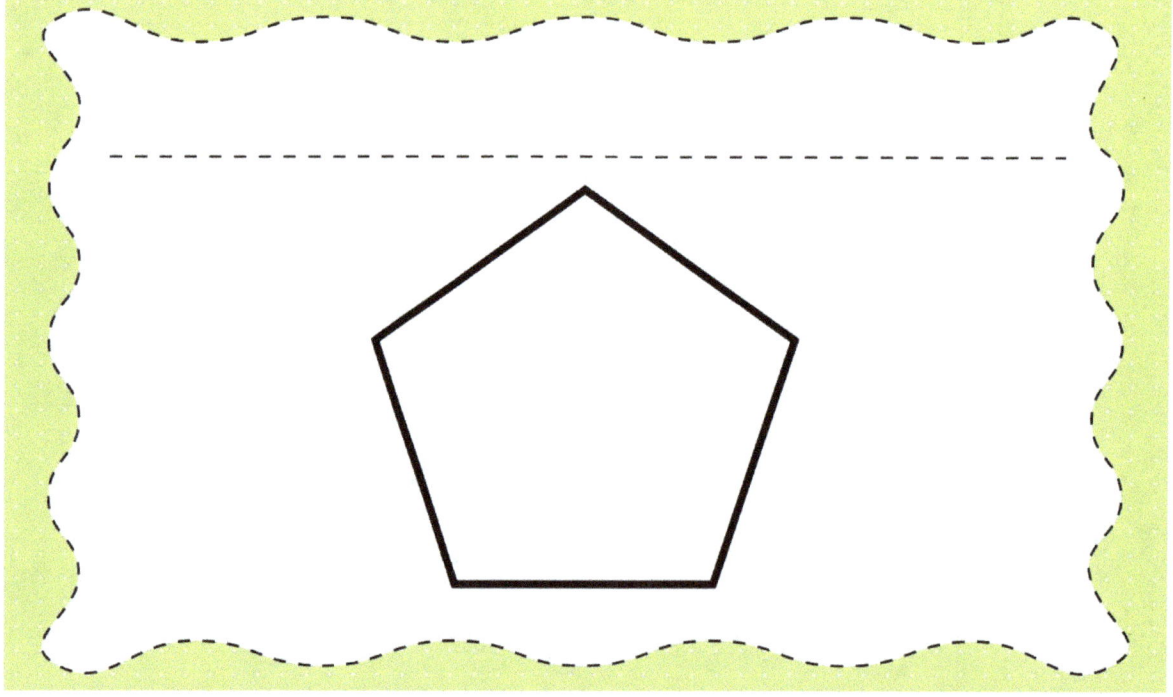

You are playing your favorite sport, and you score the winning point. Write down how you feel. Color in how intense that feeling is using green, yellow, orange, or red.

Exercise 7

Draw a picture of the happiest moment in your life.

Exercise 8

Draw a picture of the saddest moment in your life.

Exercise 9

Who is your favorite superhero? Can you draw a picture of them?

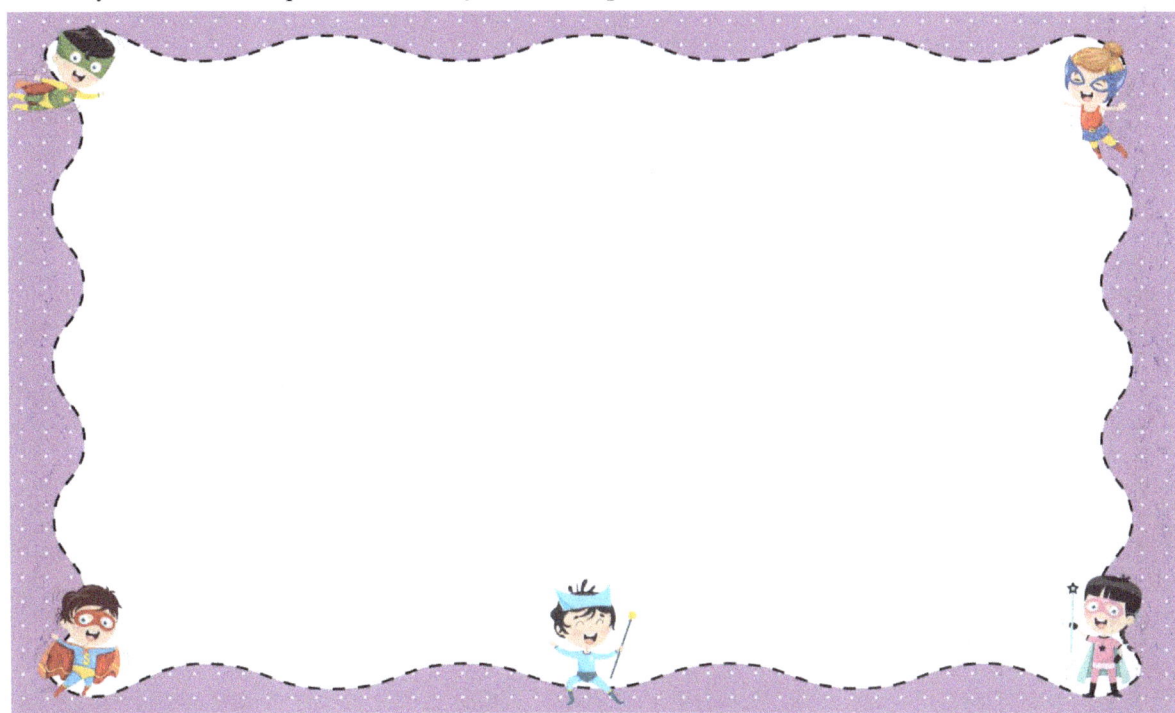

Write down what you like about them. How can you become more like your favorite superhero?

Exercise 10

When was the last time you were happy? Draw a picture of that moment.

When was the last time you were very upset? Draw a picture of that moment.

Section 2: Expressing Myself

Five Reasons It Is Important to Express Yourself

Expressing yourself means making your feelings known to the people around you.

Here are five reasons why it is good to express yourself.

- People know what you want, so they can help you if you express yourself.
- Expressing yourself helps you make friends.
- When you do not express yourself, it will make you feel worse inside.
- People will want to talk to you more because they will feel comfortable around you.
- You can learn new things when you express yourself because people will be open to teaching you.

The exercises below will help you learn how to express yourself a lot better.

Exercise 11

Art is one of the best ways to express yourself. By being creative, you can give people a look inside the inner workings of your mind.

Color in the mandala below, by using colors that match your feelings.

Exercise 12

You can express yourself by using your body. Stand up and show your friends a dance of how you are feeling right now.

Exercise 13

For the next activity, you will need some scissors, glue, paper decorations, old magazines, and an old hat. Ask your parents for help.

Cut out pictures from magazines of things that you like or that make you happy. You can even draw the picture you want to use.

Paste these pictures onto your hat to decorate it.

Now you've got a cool hat to show your friends and family what you love!

You can make a vision board, too, if you'd like! For this, you will use cardboard instead of a hat.

Find pictures of what you want to achieve by next year. Maybe you want to join the soccer team, or you want to play an instrument.

Paste the pictures on the cardboard and decorate however you want to.

Put your vision board somewhere you can see it every day to remember what you want to do and achieve.

Exercise 14

Below is a chart labeled with the five main human emotions, which are anger, fear, sadness, disgust, and enjoyment.

Close your eyes and spin your finger over the page. When you are ready, point down the chart. Whichever emotion your finger lands on, make a sound that feels like that emotion.

Remember, do not use words, *only sounds*!

Exercise 15

Some people express themselves using music.

Can you find some old things around the house to make a musical instrument like a drum or a shaker?

Musical notes are what make up a song.

https://pixabay.com/vectors/silhouette-musical-clef-bass-3275055/

Once you have your instrument, make up a song about what you are thinking or feeling right now.

You can sing the song for your family and friends if you want to.

Remember to ask your parents for permission and help before you begin.

Exercise 16

Do you know how to play pretend?

Draw a picture of what you want to be when you grow up.

Now, act out what it would be like to be the person you drew.

Exercise 17

People act in different ways when they feel different emotions or when they are thinking different thoughts. Think about how you act when you're going through different feelings.

Ask a family member or friend to help you with this activity. Below are the columns. One column says, "Looks like," the second column says, "Feels like," and the third column says, "Sounds like."

Looks like	Feels like	Sounds like

Write the words "Anger," "Fear," "Sadness," "Disgust," or "Enjoyment" on five pieces of paper. Put these pieces of paper into a bucket or a hat. Shake them up and draw one of the pieces out of the hat.

Your partner will then say, "Looks like," "Feels like," or "Sounds like." Depending on which option your partner chose, you will act out what that feeling looks like, feels like, or sounds like.

You and your partner can take turns choosing an emotion out of the hat and trying to guess the emotion.

Exercise 18

Can you think about something you can do today that will make your parents happy? Draw a picture of your parent's faces if you do this nice thing for them.

Think about what they may say to you if you do this nice thing.

Think about what you will say back to them.

Exercise 19

Can you think about something you can do today that will make your parents upset or disappointed? Draw a picture of your parent's faces if you do the thing that will make them upset.

Think about what you will say.
Think about what they may say.

Exercise 20

What is your favorite movie or TV show?

Draw a picture of your favorite character in the show.

Write down what you would say to them if you ever met them. Think about how you would feel meeting them and what you want them to know about you.

Section 3: Taming My Fears

It's okay to be scared. Fear is a natural emotion that is meant to help you protect yourself. When you are scared, your heart beats faster, and your senses, like sight and hearing, are a lot sharper. Fear is an emotion that evolved from the time when people were living in the wilderness and had to avoid predators. There are still many dangers in the modern world, so your fear is still helpful.

However, fears can turn into phobias. A phobia is when a fear no longer helps you but prevents you from doing something that could benefit you. For example, a fear of heights might stop you from going on a plane to travel the world. Therefore, you must find ways to face your fears so that they do not become a force that holds you back.

Exercise 21

To be able to face your fears, you must first discover what your fears are. What makes you scared more than anything in the world? Is it a big thunderstorm, or is it a creepy-crawly spider?

Draw a fear monster that is made up of all the things you fear the most.

Exercise 22

Many people are afraid of a lot of different things. It is okay to be scared sometimes. Write down ten things that make you feel afraid. Next to each fear, write down how scared you are on a level from 1 to 10. Writing down *10* means that you are extremely afraid, *5* means that you are at a medium level of scared, and *1* means that you are only a little bit afraid.

Fear Crusher

My Goal:

FEAR RATING SCALE

10.
9.
8.
7.
6.
5.
4.
3.
2.
1.

Exercise 23

If you want to grow into a strong person, you have to find ways to calm yourself down when you are scared. Your imagination can help you face your fears. Imagination is like a superpower that can scare you, but it can also help you not to be afraid. Just like you drew a fear monster, draw a champion who can defeat the fear monster. Think about all the things that make you feel safe and draw them with your champion.

Exercise 24

A lot of things in the world can be scary. Sometimes, things that you think are scary cannot harm you. Someone may be afraid of an earthworm, but most earthworms cannot hurt people. Draw a picture of something you are afraid of but cannot hurt you.

Ask your parents to help you with this exercise. Now, close your eyes and imagine you are sitting in a room with that fear. Think about how your body feels when you are imagining your fear so close to you.

Exercise 25

Even adults have some fears. Ask your parents or your teachers what fears they have and ask them how they face their fears. Maybe, if you are not scared of what they are scared of, you can offer to help them with their fear.

Exercise 26

Everyone needs help sometimes with the things that they fear. Ask your parents to help you with this exercise. Close your eyes and imagine something that you are scared of. How do you feel on the inside when you think about this fear? After you have imagined your fear, open your eyes and hug your parents. Do you feel better? People can help each other when someone feels scared. It is okay to speak to your parents and teachers about your fears.

Hugs can calm your fears.
https://unsplash.com/photos/MRWHSKimBJk?utm_source=unsplash&utm_medium=referral&utm_content=creditShareLink

Exercise 27

Have you ever felt so scared that it feels like your body cannot do anything? There are ways to turn down the fear inside of your body. Close your eyes and imagine something that makes you scared. Think about how your fear makes you feel. After you have imagined your fear, take a deep breath in and count to three. Then, breathe out. Take another deep breath in and then count to three, then breathe out. Repeat this ten times.

How do you feel now after doing some deep breathing? This exercise should help you control your feelings.

Exercise 28

Draw a picture of what it is like to be scared. Next to it, draw a picture of what it is like to feel safe.

How does your body feel on the inside when you are safe, and how does your body feel on the inside when you are scared?

Exercise 29

Think about the last time that you got scared. Draw a picture of the situation or object that made you afraid.

Exercise 30

Now that you have drawn a picture of what made you scared, can you draw a picture of how you got out of that scary situation?

Can you see that your fear did not last forever but only for a tiny moment? It can help to remember that when you are scared, it will not last forever. It is a feeling that will pass.

Section 4: Putting My Anger to Sleep

Everybody gets angry sometimes. Your anger shows you that you are not pleased with a situation, person, or even yourself. People sometimes do things they're not proud of when they are angry, like yelling or fighting.

Even when you are angry, it is not good to hurt people. That's why you need to find healthy ways to deal with your anger.

Exercise 31

Think about the last time you got angry. Draw a picture of what made you angry and what you did when you were angry.

Things that make people angry are called *triggers*. Can you think of some triggers that make you angry?

Exercise 32

This is called the *anger thermometer*. It helps you measure how angry you are.

At the bottom, it is cold, which means that you are not very angry. At the top, it is boiling hot, which means you are so angry it feels like you could explode.

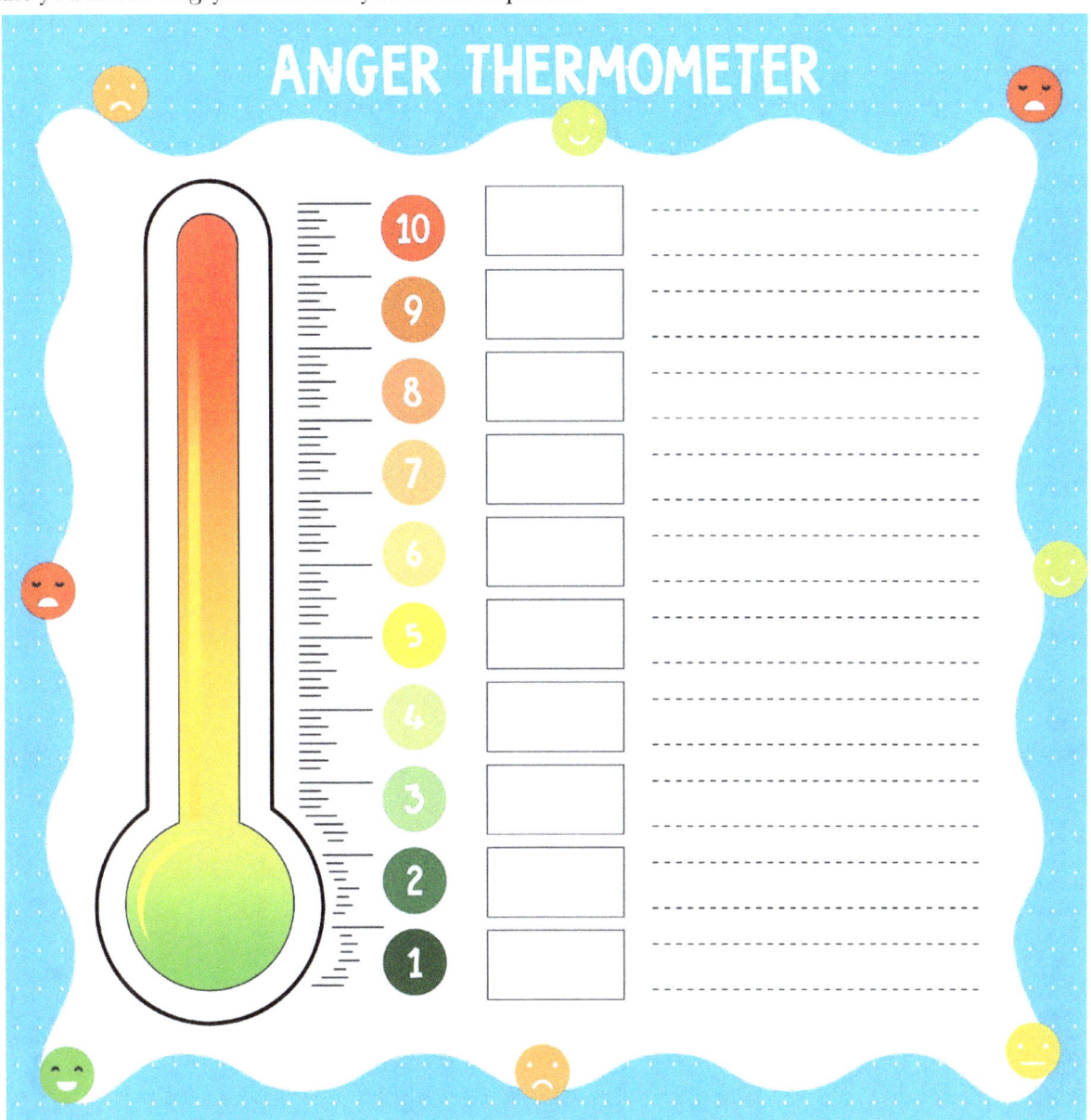

There are ten spaces next to the thermometer. Write down in each space something that makes you angry. At the bottom, write something that makes you a little angry, like maybe losing in a video game.

Then, at the top, write something that makes you extremely angry. At each level of the thermometer, you will write something that makes you angrier and angrier until you reach the highest level of anger at the top.

Exercise 33

Just because you are angry does not mean you can be rude to people or hurt them. You need to find ways to use your words when you are angry. Here are ways you can use your words to talk about your feelings.

Start your sentence with:

"I feel"

After I feel, you can describe your emotions; for example, *I feel angry.*

Once you describe your emotions, you can add "because" followed by the reason you are angry. For example, *"I feel angry because you ate my last piece of chocolate."*

Then you can ask what you would like them to do next time so that you don't get angry. For example, *"Next time, ask me before you eat my chocolate."*

Think about a time you got angry and started crying or screaming. Instead of doing that, write a sentence you could have said to communicate your feelings better.

I feel [ ] because [ ]. Next time I would like it if you [ ].

Exercise 34

Think about the last time you lost your temper. Draw a picture of how it felt right before you got angry. Maybe your chest felt hot, or you were clenching your teeth.

These are signs that you are about to lose your temper. When you feel like this, there are things you can do to calm down so that you use your words to express your anger clearly.

When you feel like this, stand up, stretch, take three deep breaths, and count to ten slowly.

Exercise 35

Physical activities can help you calm down when you are angry or frustrated. Sometimes, you need to take a break and walk away from what is making you angry.

Think about something that makes you angry. Now, go outside and run around your yard for ten laps. Come back and write down how you felt after running.

Exercise 36

Draw a picture of something that makes you happy.

Whenever you get angry, you can use your imagination to remind yourself of what makes you happy. Close your eyes and imagine this picture when you get angry. This picture is your happy place, and you can go there in your mind whenever you want to.

Exercise 37

You can use words to calm down when you are angry. The following sentences are called affirmations or mantras. These are sentences you can repeat when you feel angry or frustrated. Say these sentences out loud.

- I am calm.
- I can handle this.
- I am going to be okay.
- I am relaxed.
- I am patient.
- I can get through any situation.

Say these affirmations when you feel yourself getting angry.

Exercise 38

Draw the face of someone who is angry. Think about their eyes, mouth, and any other parts of their face.

Write down what you can do if your face looks like this.

Exercise 39

Not everyone gets angry about the same things. That's why it is important to tell people what makes you angry.

    Can you think of some things that make you angry?

    Now, think of some things that make your best friend angry.

    Think about what makes your parents and teacher angry.

    What are the differences between what makes you angry and what makes your parents angry?

Exercise 40

Color the box below with colors and patterns you think look like anger.

Now, color in this box with colors and patterns you think look like happiness.

Section 5: Keeping My Worries Away

Do you ever worry about things that are happening in your life? Maybe you have a test coming up or a big sports game you are playing. Sometimes, something terrible can happen, like your friend breaking their arm, so you worry about them.

Worrying about people and events that happen in your life is normal because it shows that you care. Worrying does not feel good and can cause you to take actions that do not help you. The following exercises will give you the tools to worry less and face challenges head-on.

Worrying does not feel good, but you can do things to help you stop worrying.
https://pxhere.com/en/photo/778587

Exercise 41

If you worry for too long, it can cause *anxiety*.

Anxiety is when you are very nervous about the future or when you worry about things that you cannot control.

Anxiety happens when you think about the future and problems too much. Your brain can paint pictures that are sometimes not real.

For this activity, you will need some glitter, a jar, and water. Pour some water and glitter into a jar. Whenever you feel like your thoughts are running away with you, shake the jar and watch the glitter slowly fall. This can help you to calm down.

Exercise 42

What causes you to worry? Draw a "worry monster" made up of all the things that make you worry.

Exercise 43

Now that you have drawn a "worry monster," draw a "worry hero" with all the things you love to do that make you calm down and feel relaxed.

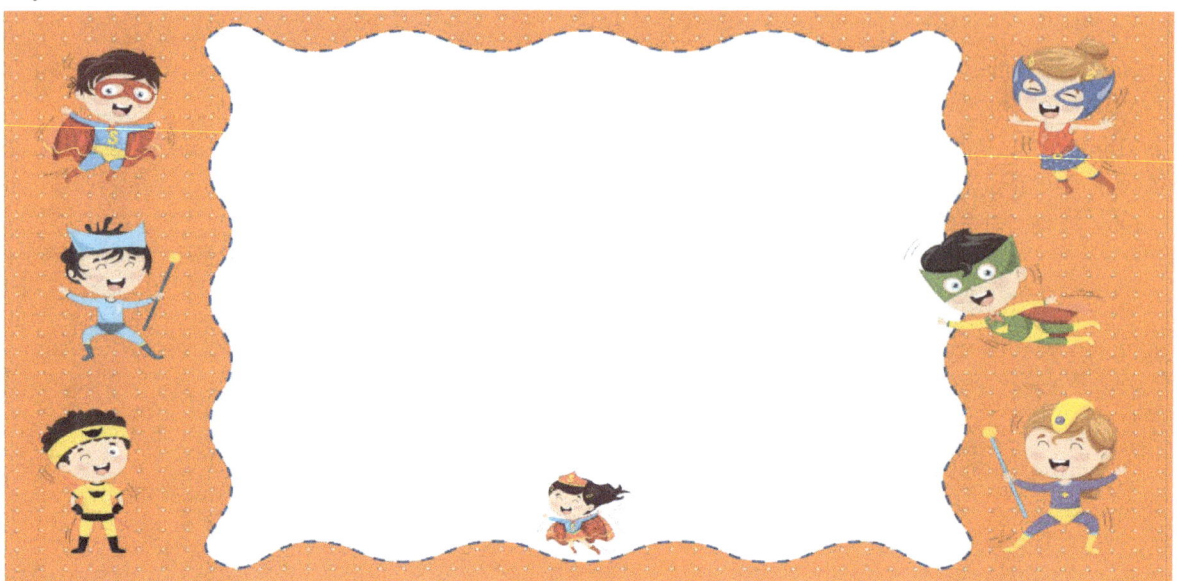

Think about which of the things you do that calm you down can help you when you are feeling worried.

Exercise 44

When you worry, often it can be because you are thinking negatively about things. Changing the way you think about problems to be more positive can help you worry less.

For example, instead of thinking, "What if I fail my test tomorrow?" you can think, "I am prepared for my test because I studied hard."

Always think positive and believe in yourself when you're studying.
https://www.pexels.com/photo/diverse-kids-studying-together-at-home-5905846/

Here are some sentences; can you write some ways to think of them positively instead?
- "Maybe my friends don't like me."
- "My mother is going to be angry because I broke a glass by mistake."
- "I am going to be late for school tomorrow."
- "I won't be able to finish my project in time for school."

Exercise 45

Do you ever feel afraid to be in your room alone? Does it feel like someone is in there watching you? Many children, and sometimes even adults, have the same worry.

Being alone in your room can be scary.
https://unsplash.com/photos/b_GtasP517U?utm_source=unsplash&utm_medium=referral&utm_content=creditShareLink

Your worries can always be decreased if you take action. Before you go to sleep, ask your parents to check your room with you. Look inside the cupboards. Look under the bed and look in all the corners of the room.

Now you will see that there is no one there, so there is no need to worry.

Exercise 46

Reading a book can stop you from worrying too much. Ask your parents to take you to the library or the bookstore to get a book you like. When you are feeling worried, take out your book to read about wonderful adventures!

Exercise 47

Journaling

Do you know what a journal is?

A journal is a book where you can write down your worries, emotions, thoughts, plans, and achievements. Some people draw or paste pictures into their journals as well.

Journaling can help you think deeper about the way you are feeling and what is making you feel that way.

Keeping a journal can also help you keep track of all the changes in your life.

Sometimes, it can be difficult to talk to people. A journal can help you get out all the thoughts that are hard to speak about out loud.

Writing in a journal every day can help you control your emotions and your behavior better.

Creating Your Journal

Ask your parents to get you a copybook journal. You can decorate this copybook with pictures, stickers, or whatever else you like.

Writing about Your Thoughts and Feelings

Every evening, or when you are feeling worried, write how you are feeling in your journal.

If you don't like writing, you can draw pictures of how you feel. This will help you to understand your worries a bit better so that you can find solutions.

Exercise 48

What makes you worry more than anything else? Write down why this makes you worry so much.

Exercise 49

Your imagination can be good for you, but it can also be bad for you. Remember that your thoughts are not always real.

Your imagination can make you more creative.
https://pixabay.com/vectors/child-drawing-childhood-imagination-5729019/

Think about something that makes you worry. Now, imagine a giant bubble surrounding that worry and carrying it far away into the sky. Take a deep breath in. How do you feel? You can use your mind to fight your worries.

Exercise 50

What do you love to do, or what is your favorite hobby? Write down a list of your hobbies, like drawing, reading, or playing outside.

Sometimes, when you are worrying, you need a break. Hobbies can distract you from your worries.

Exercise 51

How much can you count? What's the biggest number you have ever counted up to? When your thoughts feel like they are filling up your brain, start counting. Count slowly and out loud until you begin feeling better.

Section 6: Anxiety Fighters

Anxiety is when your worries build up so much that they fill your mind. This makes your body feel uncomfortable.

Anxiety can be caused by thoughts about the future or by thinking about things that you cannot control. Don't worry because there are many ways to help you deal with anxiety.

Exercise 52

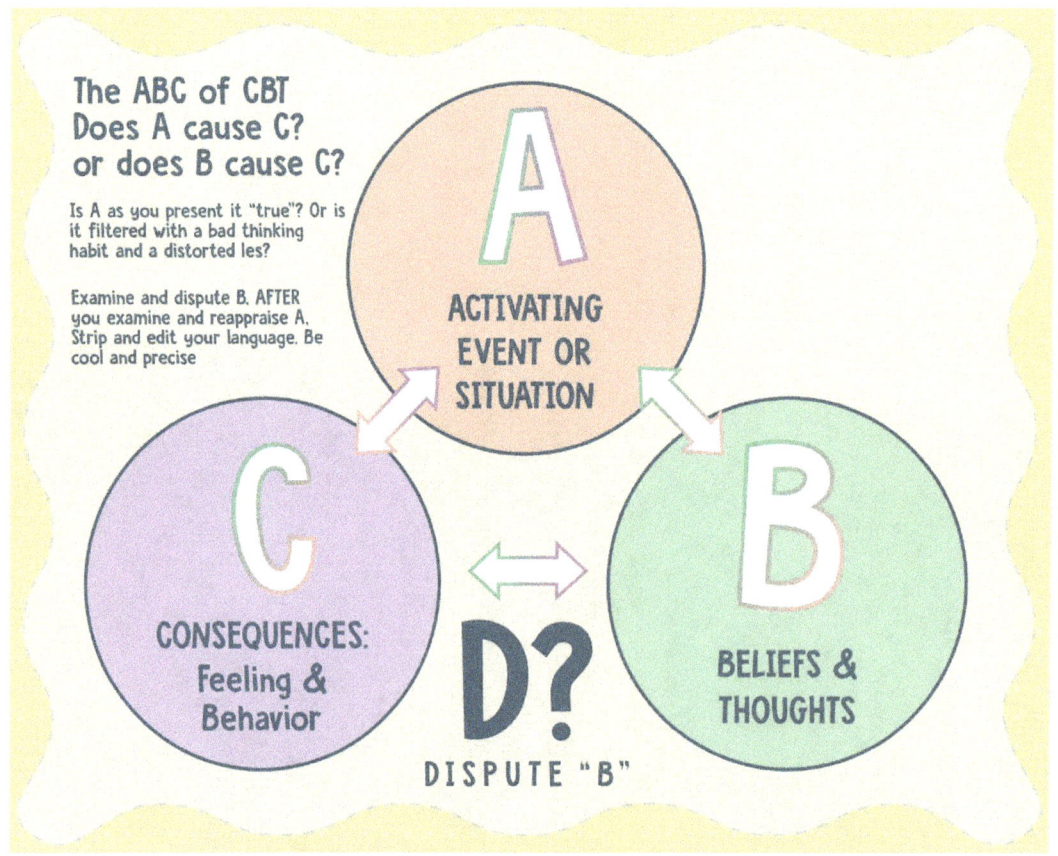

Anxiety is when you feel nervous or uncomfortable because there are too many thoughts going through your mind.

What do you do when you feel nervous?

What do you think can help you stop feeling nervous?

The ABC method is a tool that helps with anxiety. The ABC method takes your negative thoughts and turns them into positive thoughts. "A" stands for "Activating event." That means what thing happened to cause the event? "B" stands for "Beliefs about an event." "C" stands for "Consequences." Consequences are what happens after you take a certain action. For example, the consequence of eating too much sugar is cavities in your teeth.

Here's how to use the ABC method.

Start with "A" or the Activating event. Write down an event you can remember that caused anxiety.

Now "B" for "Beliefs about an event." Write down what you were thinking when the event was happening.

Finally, "C." Write down how these thoughts made you act and how they made you feel.

This exercise will help you understand why you are having certain thoughts and feelings so you can come up with better solutions.

Exercise 53

Now that you've applied the ABC method, can you write down some positive thoughts that you could have had in the same situation?

Draw a picture of your negative and positive thoughts of the same situation next to one another. Compare the two to see what changes you could have made in your mind.

Exercise 54

Let's play pretend. Imagine that you are an anxiety detective. Detectives ask people questions so they can solve problems.

Detectives use clues to solve problems.
https://pixabay.com/vectors/detective-searching-man-search-1424831/

Pretend to be a detective to ask yourself some questions. Ask yourself what makes you feel anxious and why it makes you feel anxious. This will help you find the cause of your anxiety.

Exercise 55

Talking to someone you trust about your anxieties is helpful. It is not good to keep everything bottled up. Write down a list of things that make you anxious and share that list with a parent or an adult you trust, like a teacher.

Exercise 56

Create a worry jar for your anxieties. This can help you keep track of all the thoughts and actions that cause anxiety. Certain thoughts and events that cause anxiety are known as *triggers*. By knowing your triggers, you give yourself more power to fight anxiety.

Adding your worries to a jar can help you find solutions for them.
https://unsplash.com/photos/b29z0iltxk4

Find an old jar. Whenever you are feeling anxious or having an uncomfortable thought, write it on a piece of paper and put it in the jar. At the end of the week, you can go through all the pieces of paper in the jar to find solutions and plans to help you cope with your anxiety with the help of your parents. It can be hard to think clearly when you are anxious, so this helps you think about your worries when your mind is calmer and clearer.

Exercise 57

Talking to your friends can also help you fight anxiety. Ask your parents to organize a short meeting every week to talk to a group of friends. You and your friends can share your worries and work together to tackle your anxieties over different issues. Your friends might be able to give you good advice and may even have gone through similar situations themselves.

Talking to your friends can help you find solutions to your worries.
<https://www.pexels.com/photo/children-in-circle-formation-11429489/>

Exercise 58

Can you think of your favorite smells? Maybe you like the smell of flowers or the smell of a certain type of soap. Using different scents and smells to calm you down is called *aromatherapy*.

Flowers can be used as a form of aromatherapy.
https://www.pexels.com/photo/close-up-shot-of-colorful-tulips-in-white-basket-7156469/

Get a spray bottle. Take some citrus peels and pleasant-smelling flowers and put them inside the bottle. You can even get some nice-smelling oils and add them to the mixture. After you have put the flower petals and orange peels into the spray bottle, fill it with water. Give the bottle a good, strong shake. When you spray it, a pleasant smell will come out. This smell will calm you down.

Exercise 59

Spending time outside eases anxiety. When you are indoors too often, it can feel like the walls are closing in and that your thoughts are becoming too noisy. Ask your parents to take you to a park or a nature reserve.

Walking for a little bit in a natural environment and getting some fresh air can clear your mind of negative thoughts.

Exercise 60

Touch is a great tool to help you to fight your anxiety. Next time you are feeling overwhelmed by your thoughts, take off your shoes, go outside, and stand barefoot on the sand or grass. Focus on how the ground feels in between your toes, and take a few deep breaths until you calm down.

Feeling the grass can help you calm down.
https://www.pexels.com/photo/a-person-s-feet-on-green-grass-13724474/

Exercise 61

Keeping fit and exercising also combats anxiety. Write down a list of your favorite sports. Choose one or two sports on the list that you like a lot. Ask your parents to help you find a team in your neighborhood that you can join. Maybe you could join a team at your school.

After doing all these exercises, have you learned anything new about your anxiety?

Doing sports can help you feel better.
https://www.pexels.com/photo/football-players-playing-at-field-15203/

Section 7: My Zen Zone

A *Zen zone* is a mind state where you can find calmness and peace free from anxiety, sadness, and anger. Entering a Zen zone can be done with mindfulness activities. Mindfulness exercises help you slow down your thoughts so that you can better understand yourself without too many distractions.

For most of the day, your mind works on autopilot because you are going along and reacting to what is happening around you. Mindfulness is like taking the steering wheel of your brain so that your mind is no longer driving you, but you are driving your mind.

Exercise 62

Coloring can help a lot when it comes to reducing anxiety. What types of pictures do you like to color? Below are some pictures of mandalas. Previously, you colored in a mandala with emotions on it. Now, you can color in these mandalas however you like. Use a lot of different colors and have fun!

Exercise 63

People feel their emotions in their bodies. Think about how you feel when you are angry. Maybe it feels like you are getting hot, or your heart is beating fast while your jaw is clenched. Now think about when you are happy. You may feel light and a bit tingly inside.

Doing a body scan can help you feel your emotions better. Lay down in a comfortable spot. Take a few deep breaths in and out.

With your eyes closed, bring your attention to your toes. How do they feel?

Move up to your ankles, then your knees, and then your hips. Continue up until your belly button and then to your chest and arms. Finally, bring your attention to your head. How do all the parts of your body feel? Where does it feel tight, and where is it relaxed?

Exercise 64

When you feel like your thoughts are piling up, slow your mind down with some breathing. Sit with your legs crossed and your back straight. Set a timer for five minutes. You can ask your parents to join in. Breathe in deep through your mouth and out through your nose. A lot of thoughts will pop up in your mind when you feel yourself losing focus, so bring your attention back to your breath. After five minutes of doing this, how do you feel?

Meditating with your parents can quiet your thoughts.
https://www.pexels.com/photo/mother-and-son-doing-yoga-together-6951647/

Exercise 65

Go and sit outside and close your eyes. First, start with what you are touching. What kind of chair are you sitting on? If you are on the ground, think about how the ground feels. How does your skin feel? Is it sweaty, dry, warm, or cold?

What sounds do you hear? Are there birds around? Do you hear people talking, or maybe some cars?

Think about what you can smell. Do you smell flowers or food?

Lick your lips. What can you taste? Is it sweet, sour, or bitter?

Exercise 66

A mindfulness practice that you can do easily is a room scan. Walk into your bedroom and stand in the doorway. Look around and make a list in your mind of whatever you can see.

Now leave your room and go into the kitchen. Make a list in your mind of whatever you saw in your room. Go back to your room and make a list again of what you saw. Do you see new items? What differences are there between the first time you went into your room and the second time? You can do this activity when you are feeling stressed.

Exercise 67

Do you like drawing or painting? Get a piece of paper and some paint or coloring pencils. Go sit outside and draw what you see. Maybe there is a tree or an ant hill. Take your time and draw or paint all the details. How do you feel after making your painting or drawing?

Exercise 68

Go outside for fifteen minutes and write down everything you hear. Make sure that you get permission from a grownup, or you can ask an adult to go outside with you. Do this exercise every day for about a week. Compare your lists. What differences are there? Are there any changes in what you heard? Did you hear more at the start of the week or at the end of the week?

Exercise 69

Lie down outside on a sunny day when there are some clouds in the sky. Or, at night, you can lie down on the ground and observe the stars. Ask your parents to join you. Make some shapes with the clouds, or guess what shapes the clouds look like to help you relax.

Finding shapes in the sky can help you relax.
https://www.pexels.com/photo/scenic-view-of-clouds-during-dawn-1269777/

Exercise 70

Walking is a great activity to clear your mind. Set up an obstacle course in your garden. Get cardboard and set it all around your yard. Jump from one piece of cardboard to the next. Try not to touch the ground. This is a fun game you can play with friends.

Exercise 71

Do you like music? What is your favorite song? Ask your parents to play your favorite song and make up a dance you can do together. Whenever you are feeling down, play the song and do the dance. If you want, you can make up many dances for many songs.

Dancing with your family can make you feel better.
https://www.pexels.com/photo/happy-family-dancing-4609052/

Section 8: Healthy Habits, Happy Minds

Keeping your mind and body healthy requires you to work on yourself every day.

Activities or behaviors that you repeat every day are called habits.

When you do something every day for long enough, you do not have to think about it. For example, you might brush your teeth every night before you go to bed.

Think about if you wanted to become good at playing a musical instrument. You cannot play an instrument for one day and think that you will become a great musician. You have to practice every day because you will get better slowly over time.

Good habits are activities or actions you take every day that help make you a better person. Good habits will make you healthier, smarter, and stronger, and they will let you help the people around you.

Practicing good habits every day will take you closer to being anything you want to be in life.

If you want to be happy, make friends, and do well in school, you need to think about your daily habits. These habits will include eating healthy, getting enough sleep, and having social interactions. Self-care is very important because if you feel good about yourself, you take greater actions in the world.

Exercise 72

Health is not just about your body. Health is about your emotions, your social groups, and your mind as well. Below is a wellness wheel. Each section of the wheel deals with a different part of yourself. The wheel is divided to show your emotional needs, intellectual needs, social needs, physical needs, and spiritual needs.

- Your emotional needs are everything needed to make you feel happy.
- Your physical needs are everything that makes your body healthy.
- Your social needs are everything you need from your family and friends to love them better.
- Your spiritual needs are everything that you believe in, like your religion.
- Your intellectual needs are everything that makes you smarter.

Write down what you need for each section of the wellness wheel.

Exercise 73

Planning your time can help you build healthy habits. Ask your parents to help you draw up a schedule to follow daily. This schedule should include time to do your homework, time for bed, time to wash and brush your teeth, as well as time to have fun and do chores. If you follow a schedule, you can get everything done that you need to in the day.

Exercise 74

Below is a wellness tracker.

This tracker should be filled in every day. In the first column, fill in the date.

The second column is to fill in what good things you did for yourself. This includes activities like cleaning your room or exercising.

The fourth column is to note something good you did for others, like sharing food with your friends.

The last column is for a bad habit you want to change. Maybe you left your clothes lying around, and it upsets your parents.

This can help you keep track of all of your good and bad habits so you can keep improving.

Exercise 75

Read the following sentences. Can you think of things to say to yourself when you have these negative thoughts?

- I am useless and can't do anything right.
- I am not smart enough.
- I am not good enough.
- I am always doing the wrong thing.
- I can never achieve my goals.

Thinking positively can help you succeed in all areas of your life.

Exercise 76

In the morning, when you are getting ready for school, look in the mirror and say five good things about yourself. This can be something like "I look good today" or "I am strong."

These sentences are called *affirmations*. They help you create a better mindset for yourself.

Write down five affirmations that you can repeat below.

Exercise 77

To become closer to your family or friends, you must talk to them every day. Compliments are words you say to people that make them feel good. For example, you can tell someone that they have really beautiful shoes on.

When you wake up in the morning, write down three names. These names are people that you will give compliments to when you see them. Remember to be nice to people, and people will be more polite to you.

Being kind to others will cause others to be more polite to you.
https://unsplash.com/photos/VSYVwkHT-dg?utm_source=unsplash&utm_medium=referral&utm_content=creditShareLink

Exercise 78

Being thankful is a great way to keep a healthy mind. Write down ten things you are grateful for. Maybe you are thankful that you got a good meal or that you have a warm bed. It can be an event that happened or something someone said. There is a lot to be thankful for.

Exercise 79

Eating healthy is very good for your body and mind. Write down your favorite fruits and vegetables. Every morning you can help your parents pack your lunch and remind them to add some healthy food.

Exercise 80

What do you do before you go to sleep? It is good to have a routine to clean yourself up and relax before bed. Ask your parents to help you set up a nighttime schedule. The schedule should include washing your face, brushing your teeth, putting on pajamas, and reading a book.

Exercise 81

Do you exercise? What is your favorite exercise? With the help of your parents, draw up an exercise routine to do when you have free time in the day. It will look something like this:

- 10 jumping jacks.
- 10 push-ups.
- 10 sit-ups.

Do these exercises every day with your parents.

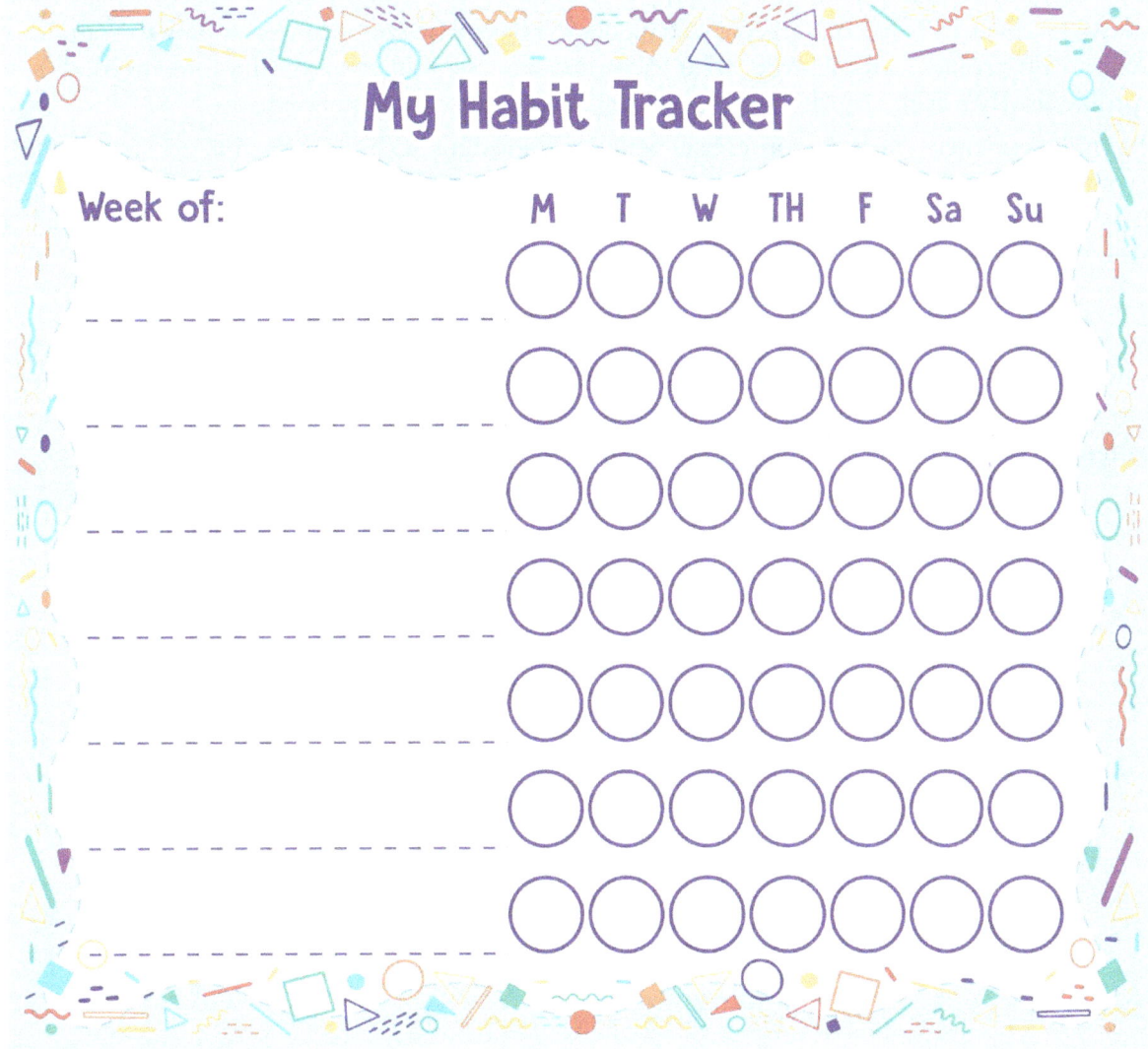

Section 9: Conquering My Biggest Challenges

In life, you will constantly encounter challenges. No matter how much your parents love you, they will not always be there to help you face your challenges. That's why you must learn how to conquer your challenges with problem-solving skills. The following exercises will give you the tools needed to solve your problems. By solving your problems, you will become more independent.

This independence will help you create better relationships with your friends and family and will help you boost your self-esteem. Self-esteem is the way you think about yourself. When you think about yourself in a positive way, you have high self-esteem. When you think about yourself in a negative way, you have low self-esteem.

Exercise 82

To know what your biggest challenges are, you first need to know what you want from your life. You need to set goals and think about where you see yourself in the future. A tool that can help point you in the right direction is a vision board.

Get a large piece of paper or cardboard. Cut out some pictures of what you want your life to be like. Maybe you want to finish school, or perhaps you want to live in a big house. Stick those pictures onto the paper or cardboard. You can write words and sentences if you want to describe them, as well. Decorate it however you like. Stick your vision board on your bedroom wall in a place where you can see it clearly. Think about what you can do every day to achieve your vision.

Exercise 83

You will face challenges daily. Sometimes the challenge will be big, and sometimes it will be small.

The table below has six columns. The first column says, "Problem of the day." Write down a challenge that you want to conquer for the day. The next three columns are "Step 1", "Step 2", and "Step 3". Break your problem into three steps that you can complete for the day. The next column says, "End result." In this column, write down what happened after you followed your three-step plan. The last column says "Improvements." In the last column, write down how you can solve the problem in a better way the next time it comes up.

Exercise 84

Positive affirmations help you face your challenges better. Below are some affirmations. Underneath each affirmation is a shape. Repeat the affirmation while coloring in the shape. Use any color that makes you happy.

I am a star.

I am whole.

I can do anything.

I can climb any mountain.

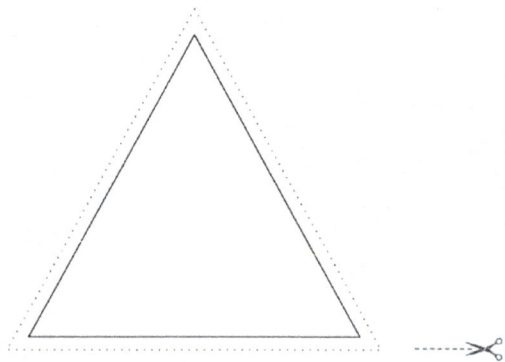

You can draw these shapes and repeat these affirmations whenever you want to.

Exercise 85

It's time to play a game of pretend. You forgot about an assignment and realized that it is due tomorrow. You have a lot of stress, and it is going to be hard work to finish the project. Your parents are there to help you with the project. The project is going to add a lot to your grades, so you must get it done. Can you write down the best ways that you can solve the problem?

Exercise 86

Being out of a soccer game doesn't mean you can't be supportive.
https://www.pexels.com/photo/action-ball-field-game-274506/

You are in a soccer match, and you hurt yourself. The coach takes you out of the game and puts you on the bench. The score is still 0-0, but your team has a good chance of winning. You are upset and angry that you are on the bench. Write down some ways that you can support your team from the sidelines. Also, write down ways in which you can control your emotions to manage your feelings about being taken off the field.

Exercise 87

Your parents have taken away your favorite toy, tablet, or video game as a punishment because you were misbehaving. You are upset and sitting in your room bored. Write down some ways that you can manage your emotions. Also, think about how you can prevent yourself from being bored. Now, write down some ways you can make your parents happy so that they can give you back your toy, tablet, or video game.

Exercise 88

Can you think of any problems you faced in the past? Write down the problem and how you overcame it.

Write down the worst thing that could have happened if the problem continued.

Now, write down the *best thing* that could have happened if you solved the problem better.

Think about future problems. In the future, how can you apply what you learned in this problem?

Exercise 89

Draw a picture of where you see yourself by the end of the year. This has to be the best possible version of yourself if you achieve all your goals, like getting good grades or making new friends.

Think about how you can make sure that that version of yourself exists in the future. What habits can you change? What habits can you start? What decisions can you make daily?

Exercise 90

Ask your parents to help you set up a scavenger hunt. Your parents should hide a toy somewhere in the yard. Around the house, they should write down some clues about where the toy is.

Once the scavenger hunt is set up, you can use your problem-solving skills to figure out the clues and find the hidden item.

You can do this with your friends as well. You and your friends can take turns setting up a scavenger hunt for each other.

Exercise 91

This is a competition where you can play against your friends. Ask your parents to get you some glue and sticks. These sticks can be toothpicks, match sticks, or ice cream sticks. You and your friends can divide into two or three teams. You must work together to build a tall tower out of sticks and glue. Whoever builds the tallest tower wins.

Section 10: Embracing Myself

Nobody is perfect. Everybody has flaws, and everybody makes mistakes. Some people put their clothes on backward, and other people have smelly feet. Some people talk way too loudly, and others whisper super softly. No matter the flaws you have or the mistakes you make, you are still worth so much in the world! Accepting yourself with all your imperfections is how you can build high self-esteem. Your self-esteem and self-image come from the way you think about yourself.

No one is going to love you more than you love yourself. No one will spend more time with you than yourself because you live inside your body. That's why you need to make sure that you love and care for yourself, even in times when you are feeling low.

Exercise 92

Here is a list of 20 different positive traits. Circle the traits that you feel best describe you and your personality.

1. Kind
2. Strong
3. Hard-working
4. Humble
5. Beautiful
6. Fast
7. Athletic
8. Intelligent
9. Caring
10. Loving
11. Friendly
12. Funny
13. Neat
14. Brave

15. Curious
16. Charming
17. Interesting
18. Creative
19. Unselfish
20. Adventurous

Now that you've circled some of these characteristics, you should draw a picture of yourself that represents these traits.

Exercise 93

Now that you have circled some of the positive traits mentioned above, can you think of other positive characteristics about yourself?

It's important to remind yourself of your positive traits.

https://unsplash.com/photos/g3KbcDWrBUM?utm_source=unsplash&utm_medium=referral&utm_content=creditShareLink

Write down some positive things about yourself with some colorful pens and stick them on a mirror. Every time you look in that mirror, remind yourself how amazing you are!

Exercise 94

Sometimes, it can be difficult to think of good things to say about yourself. Ask your friends and family what they like about you. Write down what they said to remember that there are people in your life who love you and think that you are incredible.

Exercise 95

A support system is the people that help you in your life. This can be your friends, family, and your teachers. Below is a tree with some empty spaces for names. This is your support system tree. Write down all the people who care about you in the empty spaces provided.

Exercise 96

Ask your parents if you can decorate your notebook or journal. This book will be your compliment journal. Decorate the book with whatever you want. This can be pictures of stuff that you like or with your favorite colors. Every day, in the morning, write a compliment to yourself. *A compliment is something that you like about yourself.* This can remind you that you are a person who should be treated well and who can achieve anything you set your mind to.

Exercise 97

Reminding yourself of your strengths can help you become more confident.
https://unsplash.com/photos/_XTY6lD8jgM?utm_source=unsplash&utm_medium=referral&utm_content=creditShareLink

Think about what you are good at. This can be a sport or even a subject at school. It may even be a video game that you are good at. Write down why you are so good at this activity and how you can become better at it.

Exercise 98

Think of a victory dance that you can do when you win a game or achieve something great. Show your victory dance to your friends and family. Whenever you succeed at something, do this victory dance to celebrate.

Exercise 99

Can you think of a moment in the past when you did something great or achieved one of your goals? It is amazing that you were able to do that! Draw a picture of the moment when you achieved something great in the past.

Exercise 100

One of the ways you can boost your confidence is by doing a power pose. This is the pose that superheroes do when they arrive to defeat the bad guy! Whenever you are feeling down or weak, do this pose. Stand up tall. Spread your legs wide, then raise your right fist into the sky as high as you can. Do you feel the power?

Exercise 101

Ask your parents for some old magazines and newspapers. Think about all your strengths and the things that make you great. Now, cut out some pictures that represent those strengths and stick them onto a poster. Look at that poster whenever you feel down or are doubting yourself.

Bonus Section: Thought Challenge

This bonus section is the final exercise in the book.

Congratulations! You have worked through all the exercises and are on your way to making your life so much better. The final exercise is a checklist for you to work through daily. This checklist will show you how well you are doing and whether you are sticking to the lessons you've worked through in the book. This checklist should be done at the end of every day as a way to track your progress and your daily activities.

Checklist

☐ Did I think about how I feel today?

☐ Did I do something nice for myself today?

☐ Did I feel anxious at any time during the day?

☐ Did I implement any of the tools I learned in this book to help with my anxiety?

☐ Did I lose my temper today?

☐ Did I use any of the tools in the book to control my anger?

☐ Did I say something nice to my friends today?

☐ Did I say something nice to my family today?

☐ Did I stick to my schedule?

☐ Did I eat healthily today?

☐ Did I get more than 8 hours of sleep last night?

☐ Have I worked on my physical health today?

☐ Have I worked on my mental health today?

☐ Have I worked on my social needs today?

☐ Have I worked on my spiritual needs today?

- ☐ Did I write down anything in my journal today?
- ☐ Have I done anything today to reach the goals on my vision board?
- ☐ Have I worked on addressing any bad habits today?
- ☐ Have I done any mindfulness exercises today?
- ☐ Have I conquered any fears today?
- ☐ Did I have fun today?
- ☐ Was today a good day or a bad day?
- ☐ Did I talk to myself in a positive way today?
- ☐ Have I spent time in nature or outside today?
- ☐ Have I done any physical activities today?

Thank You

Thank you so much for completing all the activities in this book! You are now one step closer to becoming the best version of yourself that can change the world! Remember that you are valuable and that it is important to love and care for yourself. Continue working hard through these exercises because these can be applied throughout your life. Thank you for caring enough about yourself to put in the work that can help you achieve your goals and dreams.

When you look in the mirror, you should also be grateful that you are committed enough to complete the project of working on yourself. With the help of these activities, all your mental, physical, and emotional needs will be fulfilled. Say, *thank you* to the person who bought this book for you. They care about you very much and have started you on an exciting adventure of self-discovery.

Check out another book in the series

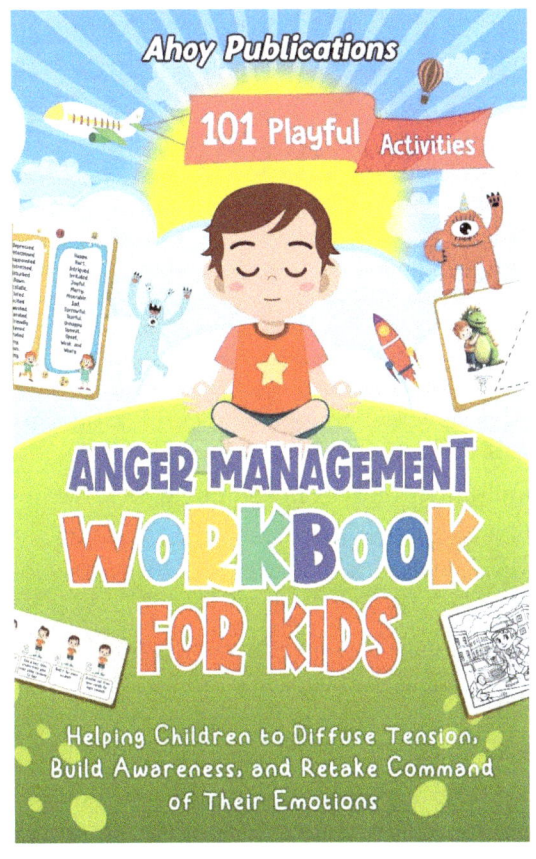

References

(N.d.). Gov.au. https://www.cci.health.wa.gov.au/-/media/CCI/Consumer-Modules/Back-from-The-Bluez/Back-from-the-Bluez---04---The-ABC-Analysis.pdf

Aid, T. (2019, May 28). Using imagery in CBT. Therapist Aid. https://www.therapistaid.com/therapy-guide/using-imagery-in-cbt

Anxiety and fear in children. (n.d.). Gov.au. https://www.betterhealth.vic.gov.au/health/conditionsandtreatments/fear-and-anxiety-children

Elaine Houston, B. S. (2019, June 17). CBT for children: A guide for helping kids in therapy. Positivepsychology.com. https://positivepsychology.com/cbt-for-children/

Halder, S., & Mahato, A. K. (2019). Cognitive behavior therapy for children and adolescents: Challenges and gaps in practice. Indian Journal of Psychological Medicine, 41(3), 279–283. https://doi.org/10.4103/ijpsym.ijpsym_470_18

Hirschlag, A. (2018, December 18). How to cope with anxiety: 13 simple tips. Healthline. https://www.healthline.com/health/mental-health/how-to-cope-with-anxiety

Nunez, K. (2020, April 17). ABC model of cognitive behavioral therapy: How it works. Healthline. https://www.healthline.com/health/abc-model

Rodriguez, J. (2019, April 10). How journaling benefits your child. Scholastic.com; Scholastic Parents. https://www.scholastic.com/parents/books-and-reading/raise-a-reader-blog/how-journaling-benefits-your-child.html

Ruini, C., & Mortara, C. C. (2022). Writing technique across psychotherapies—from traditional expressive writing to new positive psychology interventions: A narrative review. Journal of Contemporary Psychotherapy, 52(1), 23–34. https://doi.org/10.1007/s10879-021-09520-9

Walter, I. R. (2017, October 10). 10 therapist (and child)-approved activities to support kids with anxiety —. Family Therapy Basics. https://familytherapybasics.com/blog/2017/10/8/10-therapist-and-child-approved-activities-to-support-kids-with-anxiety

www.ingramcontent.com/pod-product-compliance
Lightning Source LLC
Chambersburg PA
CBHW060414010526
44107CB00006B/688